Remembering A Son

Remembering John

Patrick H. Munley

INFINITY PUBLISHING

Copyright © 2011 by Patrick H. Munley

ISBN 0-7414-6526-4

Printed in the United States of America

Published July 2011

INFINITY PUBLISHING
1094 New DeHaven Street, Suite 100
West Conshohocken, PA 19428-2713
Toll-free (877) BUY BOOK
Local Phone (610) 941-9999
Fax (610) 941-9959
Info@buybooksontheweb.com
www.buybooksontheweb.com

Dedication

The loss of a child is one of the most heartbreaking and painful losses families may endure. This book is dedicated to all parents, brothers, sisters and family members of children who died much too young and to The Compassionate Friends, a worldwide organization, dedicated to helping families cope with this heartrending loss.

Table of Contents

Chapter 1

Family

Mary Anne and I met during our college years at Seton Hall University in South Orange, New Jersey. She was a freshman, and I was a senior. The year was 1968, a tumultuous time... the Vietnam War was raging in Southeast Asia, the Civil Rights movement was creating fault lines around the country, the nation was stunned by the assassination of Martin Luther King and Robert Kennedy, riots erupted in the City of Newark, neighboring South Orange, and in other cities around the country; antiwar and civil rights protests and demonstrations were commonplace. The call for involvement and commitment to making the world better a place never seemed stronger. When we met, Mary Anne was a volunteer tutor for the East Orange public schools and I was a tutor for a program sponsored by Volunteers in Service to America (VISTA) in the inner city of Newark. Volunteers for each program were recruited and sponsored in part by the University's Social Action Committee. The Committee, initiated by students during the late 1960's sponsored special community projects and programs intended to help disadvantaged youth in surrounding communities.

Mary Anne and I were married in a beautiful service on June 5, 1971 at the Seton Hall Chapel surrounded by our friends and family. The songs of the wedding offered the promise of a wonderful future – from Beethoven's Ode to Joy; to West Side Story's One Hand, One Heart; to Handel's Messiah. We had both wanted a large family. In a special way children seemed to offer hope for bringing into the world people who would help transform the world, who would live on after us and continue to strive to make the world a better place, the kind of place we all would like to envision.

To a wonderful extent the dream happened. We were blessed as a family with five wonderful children: Elizabeth Anne, Thomas Edward, Michael Patrick, John Patrick and Katherine Claire. Mary Anne worked as a full-time mother when the children were growing up and later entered her chosen career as an early childhood teacher. I worked as a psychologist during my early career and served on the staff of several VA Medical Centers on the East Coast before moving to Battle Creek MI to become Chief of Psychology Service in 1984.

When we moved to Michigan we were fortunate enough to find a wonderful home in a lovely neighborhood with a very large wooded backyard. The property contained over 50 oak trees, bordered by a picturesque pond and stream, with a land bridge across to neighbors on the other side. When we found our Michigan home and I first saw the picturesque setting I realized how lucky we were. This was the kind of home and place where we could live the rest of our lives, and never feel the need to move again. It was an idyllic setting for the children to grow up in. The best of both worlds: a suburban neighborhood with quiet streets where they could play with friends, safely ride their bicycles; and a rural backyard full of trees, a pond and a stream for fishing and canoeing, and lots of fun. The children spent countless hours growing-up by the pond: fishing, canoeing, catching turtles and frogs, and going on adventures of exploration down the stream with each other and their friends. We all liked the outdoors in the summer time.

Ours became a family of swimmers. Each of the children was an age group swimmer when they were young. We had encouraged each of the children to become involved in swimming at a young age. Swimming was one sport, where if a young person practiced, worked hard and put forth the effort, they would make the high school team. They would have the positive life-experience of being part of a team; learning to accomplish individual and team goals as a part of their sport. At the high school level swimming is a great sport, since it is inclusive of all young people who are motivated to try and give their best effort. All of the children were members of the Portage Central High School swim team. For more than a decade, there was always at least one Munley swimming for the school: Elizabeth from 1987 to 1990, Thomas from 1988 to 1992, Michael from 1991 to 1995, John from 1993 to 1997, and Katie from 1996 to 1999. And each of the children also spent at least one year as team captain.

After high school, most of the children stopped swimming competitively. Elizabeth went on to complete her undergraduate degree in social relations from James Madison College at Michigan State University. Michael went to the University of Michigan, where he earned a BA in economics and went on to work for the Federal Reserve Bank in Chicago as an economist. Katie went on to Arizona State University where she graduated from the Walter Cronkite School of Broadcast Journalism. Thomas and John, however, both continued to swim and both achieved great things in the pool. Thomas went on to Michigan State University, where he was an All-American, Honorable Mention in the 200-yard freestyle in 1996. He graduated with a BA and MBA in accounting and went to work as a business consultant. John, following his older sister and brother's footsteps went to Michigan State, where he majored in Packaging and swam for MSU from 1997 to 2001. Thomas's success in the pool was not surprising. He'd long been a successful swimmer. But John's success, given his fun-loving personality and the trajectory of his early career as a swimmer, was remarkable.

Chapter 2

John Patrick

John was born on Wednesday, April 11, 1979 at 11:45 p.m. at St. Clare's Hospital in Denville New Jersey weighing 9 lbs. 1 oz.. He was a very healthy baby. His brothers and sister all wanted their new baby brother to come home in time for Easter. So Mary Anne and I brought him home on Easter Sunday, wearing a Snoopy stretch suit that his older brother Thomas picked out for him. Waiting in his bassinet was a stuffed rabbit, one of his earliest friends who slept with him every night until he was 5. John fit right into the family.

Since he was born in April he ended up going to the pool everyday during his first summer. He took naps in his baby carriage under a tree by the swimming pool where his older brothers and sister swam and played. He loved the water from an early age. When John was four years old, Mary Anne had to take Katie to the doctor for an appointment. She left John at the pool in the care of her older cousins, Catherine Roche and Sister Jeremiah, who had volunteered to baby sit and watch the kids at the pool for the afternoon. Mary Anne's cousins were never swimmers themselves, and had little knowledge of the kids' swimming abilities. Mary Anne assumed John would remain in the shallow-end of the pool where she had left him.

John, however, was always adventurous from a very young age. He told Catherine and Sister that he wanted to go off the high diving board at the pool and that he "did this all the time". He talked Catherine and Sister Jeremiah into letting him go to the deep end of the pool where the diving boards were located and all the older kids were jumping off the boards. When Mary Anne returned a few hours later and walked into the swimming pool area– there was John standing at the end of the high diving board. As she called out to him he jumped off the high board into the pool and promptly swam to the ladder to exit the pool. When Mary Anne asked her cousins why in the world were they letting a four-year old jump off the high dive they told her that John had said "Mommy lets me do this and I do this all the time". In actuality he had never done it before.

John began school at St. Joseph's School in West Orange, New Jersey. He was not really fond of kindergarten and at first asked "Why did they need to worry about all those letters?" All he really wanted to do was to stay home and build with his Legos. In the middle of his kindergarten year our family moved to Michigan. This was his first plane trip and he was a little nervous. He wondered aloud "How could that big airplane stay up in the sky?" But ended up fascinated by the experience and spent the entire trip looking out the window. In Michigan he entered Woodland Elementary School. Upon returning home from the first day of kindergarten Mary Anne asked him how school was, and John replied "Great!" When she asked him what made school so great he answered, "They have letters all over the floor and they don't even care about them!"

Throughout his elementary school years John loved to play outside in the woods and pond in our backyard. He spent countless hours catching turtles and frogs, fishing, canoeing and going on wonderful adventures. He loved animals and loved watching and feeding the geese and ducks that visited the pond and woods. When he was in the second grade he befriended a wild duck that he named "Quackers". John would go outside from the house, bring a handful of crackers and call out for "Quackers". The duck would come up to him and eat out of the palm of his hand. When her ducklings were born she would bring her ducklings with her to feast on the stale bread and cereal that John would provide. He also loved the dogs we had at home over the years, particularly Thomas's golden retriever, Relay. When John was in high school and his brother Thomas was off at college Relay, would always sleep on the foot of John's bed.

As John grew up, he was always his own person: independent, assertive, very comfortable making his own decisions and being on his own. He struggled somewhat academically, in elementary school and high school, and seemed to have a mild learning disability. He didn't like the academic part of school very much and struggled with his writing and spelling. When he was a senior in high school he came home one evening and at the dinner table talked about how his English teacher wanted him to write a poem. He told us how he hated poetry and that he didn't want to do the assignment. We encouraged him to follow through on the assignment, which he did, but he didn't tell us what he wrote. Only later did we learn that the poem he wrote was selected for inclusion in Montage, the high school literary magazine. The title of his poem was simply "I hate it" and consisted of a humorous listing of things that he didn't like and concluded with: "Most of all I hate poetry." The poem was vintage John.

While John struggled in some academic subjects he excelled with technology and computers. He was always putting together things and taking them apart. He loved video games, computers and Nintendo. He subscribed to National Geographic and loved to read books on how things worked. He also loved many sports besides swimming. When he was young he played little league baseball, soccer and took up diving for a brief period in middle school. He even won the middle school diving championship. He was a founding member of the Portage Central water polo team. He would also play Frisbee golf whenever he had a chance. But swimming was his true love.

John was not heavily recruited as a swimmer out of high school. His times were very good in high school but not great. His brother Thomas saw his potential, though, and told

Coach Bader at MSU that he should recruit John, because John, Thomas said, was going to be better than he had been and most people didn't realize it. Coach Bader took Thomas' advice and recruited John. He worked and trained very hard in college and went on to do very well at Michigan State University. He served as team co-captain, was ranked nationally in the 200-yard freestyle, set the Michigan State University Record in the 200-yard freestyle and qualified to swim at the 2000 Olympic trials in Indianapolis.

As part of his preparation for the Olympic trials John swam for two summers with Club Wolverine in Ann Arbor, MI. There he trained with Coach Jon Urbancek, who at the time was a coach for the US Olympic Swim Team and Head Coach at the University of Michigan. John went to the US Olympic Training Center in Colorado. He swam those two summers with some of the best swimmers in the world including Tom Malchow, gold medalist in the men's 200 butterfly at the 2000 Sydney Olympics and world record holder in the 200 butterfly in 2000; Eric Namesnik, two-time Olympic silver medalist in the 400-meter individual medley; Mark Leonard All-American swimmer; Joe Tristan, ranked in the Top 20 in the world in the 200 meter freestyle; Garrett Mangieri, an NCAA All-American. These were some of the best swimmers in the world at the time. John teamed up with Tom Malchow, Joe Tristan, and Garrett Mangieri to set the University of Michigan pool record in the 800-meter relay. Although John had not qualified for the Olympic team, he would not let Tom Malchow and his relay teammates forget how lucky they were that he was there to carry the relay team to set the pool record.

When John was in college and swimming for Michigan State University he decided the swim team needed a mascot. So he took a portion of his scholarship money allotted for room and board and went to Meijer and bought a life size ceramic golden retriever, which he named Winston. He took Winston with him to practice and swim meets. During swim meets John would put Winston up on the high diving board, high above the pool, to oversee the meet. John even took Winston with him when the MSU swim team had their team picture taken, and Winston was included in the picture and is seen sitting as part of the team. While I was appalled that he had taken some of his scholarship money to do this, that was John. He enjoyed himself, he had fun and he had a great sense of humor.

When Thomas went off to Michigan State and began swimming at the college level the family would often go to meets as often as possible. One of the noticeable things about college swimmers was that many of the swimmers would have tattoos. This was not commonplace at the high school level, but was very common for college swimmers, men and women both. Whenever Thomas came home from college during his freshman year his brothers and sisters would often ask him "When are you going to get your tattoo?" I always made my position as father quite clear that I didn't like tattoos; I didn't think they were appropriate, and I was completely opposed to Thomas getting a tattoo. Well not so much because I was opposed to tattoos as because Thomas himself didn't wish to get one, Thomas never got a tattoo.

Similarly, when John joined the MSU swim team and he would come home for the occasional weekend visit his siblings would ask him when he was going to get his tattoo. I, again of course, made my position clear. At Easter dinner during John's freshman year, John and the whole family were gathered around the dinner table. Elizabeth asked: "Well John, when are you going to get your tattoo?" John replied: "Well, actually it will not be that long at all?" At that moment, everyone at the dinner table realized John had gotten a tattoo. All of his brothers and sisters broke out laughing and insisted on seeing the tattoo. In response John stood up at the dinner table, unbuckled his belt and pulled down the right side of his trousers to show everyone his tattoo of a green frog on the front of his right hip, in a spot that would be partially covered by his bathing suit. While his brothers and sisters roared with laughter. I could not believe my eyes. All I could think of was why in the world would he get a tattoo. Not wanting to make too big of a scene at the dinner table, after all it was Easter and we were celebrating his birthday, all I could manage to say was "John, why in the world did you get a tattoo of a frog? This is like having a brand new silver BMW, painting a green frog on the side, and ruining a new BMW. Why in the world would you do something like this?" John just smiled. I didn't get it, but he was happy and didn't wish to explain.

Two years later I attended the MSU Swim Team awards dinner in April of 2000. I had traveled from a conference earlier in the day and arrived in time for the awards dinner held at the student union on the campus of MSU. Over 250 people were in attendance. John and I sat together at a table in the center of the gathering for dinner. When the awards were presented, John was called up to receive the Most Valuable Swimmer Award. As John stood next to Coach Bader in front of the attendees, Coach discussed John's accomplishments and contributions for the team during the season. As he continued he said that John really stood out in terms of his Spartan Spirit. Coach went on to tell the story about how John, when training with Club Wolverine at the University of Michigan the previous summer, was thrown out of the weight training room for wearing his Michigan State T-shirt into the weight room. Coach said that John responded by getting a tattoo of a Spartan S on his hip and told the staff at the U of M that they would not be able to make him take this Spartan S off. For a moment as I was listening to the story I was in a state of confusion, the coach was wrong, John's tattoo was of a green frog, not a Spartan S, what was he talking about .....Then John leaned over to the microphone and said: "Coach, my father does not know about this tattoo yet." And John looked in my direction and smiled, and everyone at the dinner turned to look at me for my reaction and all I could do was try to smile.

John's senior year was not without its challenges. At the end of October John was riding his bike home from practice and rode over what he thought was a pile of leaves only to have the bike fall in the hole that the leaves were covering. John fell off his bike and hurt his knee. It slowed him down a bit but he had a goal and a sore knee wasn't going to stop him. This was his senior year, his last year of college swimming. He didn't worry about academics because he knew he had the rest of his life to make his mark in packaging but only 4 months left to achieve his goal in swimming. The Big Ten Swimming Championships were held at the University of Minnesota that year and Mary Anne and I decided to go. John swam the 500 free and qualified 11th and then in the finals finished 9th winning the consolation heat in the 3rd fastest time in the history of MSU swimming. Friday was his day, the day of the 200 free. John qualified in the top 8 to swim in the championship heat that night. That night John finished 3rd setting a new record at MSU. The 800 free relay was less than an hour later and John asked the coach to let him lead off so that he could get the team off to a good start. John led off and broke his own record! What a great night to see the smile on his face of having achieved his goal. John also met with success professionally that spring having been offered a very well paying internship in packaging. On April 21 at the awards banquet John accepted the Most Valuable Swimmer award for the fourth time in as many years at MSU.

Everyone who knew John seems to have their own favorite stories about him. Coach Matt Gianiodis, Assistant swim coach when John was at MSU tells a couple of stories about John.

"You know when head Coach Richard Bader was busy and he would say Munley wants to go to some meet- we got the money, so just take him down to San Antonio or take him to Minneapolis or wherever. So we would go there and then the coaches would be like, 'Hey G, How is your boy going to do this week? Is he going to do all right?' And I would say,

'I have, well you know, I have no idea.' And that was John –
you were not quite sure what he was going to do or say, he
would always surprise you. When I started coaching at
Michigan State, John had already started practicing with the
team. One day I realized that when John was training he
always wore his swim suit so low that you would see the
crack of his rear end because the suit was so low. But then at
the swim meets he would hike his suit almost up to his belly
button. So one day I called over one of the guys on the team
and said: 'what's the deal with Munley, what's the deal with
that ass and his swim suit? Is he putting on some kind of
ritual or what? The guy says, 'No his dad doesn't know that
he has the tattoo and John is hiding the tattoo when his
parents are at the meet.' About six months later I hear that
his parents found out about the tattoo. I asked John what his
father said and John replied: "Well we were at the dinner
table and my dad comes down and is all flustered and he
says, 'I just don't understand, you have a BMW and you
paint a green frog on the side of it – it doesn't make any
sense.' I told John, 'You know John; he could've called you a
Yugo'. John just laughed.

Coach Gianiodis also recalled when he took John and
another swimmer to a swim meet featuring Big Ten All-Stars
versus the Olympians in Chicago:

"So we all drove down to Chicago, me, Bruesch, and
Munley, they had a meet about two or three years ago, an all-
star meet. And John had decided that he wanted to swim the
100 yard freestyle. So this all-star meet was made up of the
best athletes in the Big 10 and from around the country. But
anyway, John gets in this heat of the 100 yard freestyle and
he's seeded last in the heat and he is all the way down in lane
8. The heat has some of the fastest freestyle sprinters in the
country. And as an all all-star meet, they made a big deal and
had all the pomp and circumstance of a championship meet
with formal introductions of everyone in the field. And as
they're going down introducing the line-up of swimmers in
the heat they give their bio and swimming accomplishments

– like 'in lane 4 Joe Smith, former world record holder in the 50 freestyle, lane 3, former Olympian and NCAA champion in the 50 freestyle' and all the guys in the heat had résumés. Except when they then get to John and all the announcer says is 'lane 8 John Munley Michigan State University'. ... Well, let me tell you that John went out and had an incredible swim and won the race. So he then gets out of the water, and is walking back to join us when he walks by Coach Jon Urbanchek, who was then Head Coach at the University of Michigan and Head Coach of the United States Olympic team. Coach Urbanchek calls out to John, "Hey Munley that was a great swim. I had no idea you could go that fast" and John looks at him and says, "I know, that's why I went to Michigan State." I am sitting there and I hear this and I couldn't believe it – with all the all-stars and Olympic swimmers around John is saying this to the Head Olympic Coach – but that was John, always surprising you with his tongue in cheek sense of humor."

Katie remembers the time she and John went back to New Jersey for the summer to stay with friends, to work and to have some fun. During the summer Katie spent quite a bit of time babysitting to make some extra money for herself. She earned $88 which was quite a bit of money for her as a 12 year old. Upon their return to Michigan Katie was trying to decide how to spend her hard earned money from the summer. She really wanted an American Girl doll, however, John told her how much more fun she would have with a Nintendo instead. Following John's advice she decided to buy the Nintendo with her money and asked me to purchase one for her. I brought her home the Nintendo, she took out her polka dot wallet and handed me the $88. As soon as the transaction was completed John grabbed the Nintendo, took it downstairs, hooked it up and began playing with it as Katie immediately realized the error of her ways.

Elizabeth's husband Doug remembers family pictures with John. As the kids grew up, John's older sister and brothers would often bring home dates around the holidays or special occasions. On these special occasions, we would like to have a picture taken of the family and everyone who was present at the gathering. Whenever one of his older brothers or sisters had a date who was present for the picture, John would always insist that the date stand at the far right or left side of the group. When asked why, he would explain that he didn't want a perfectly good family picture ruined, after his brother or sister and the guest they were dating broke-up at some point in the future. John would simply say that if they were standing at the end of the line in the picture they could be easily cut out of the picture and we would still have a good family picture left. This was why often in some of our family pictures, future and eventual brother-in-law's and sisters-in- law are seen standing at the far right hand side or left-hand side of the picture because they had been guided to this position by John.

One exception to John's picture rule was Michael's wife, Stephanie. She came to dinner when they were dating and had been warned beforehand of John's rule, but when everyone lined up for a picture, she gamely stood on the inside of Michael. Doug and others told to move to the outside, but John surprised everyone by saying, "No. She's OK. She can stay." He seemed to know before anyone else that Stephanie would become a part of our family. In fact, one of his favorite discussion topics was when is Michael going to propose to Stephanie.

One of my favorite stories is the story told by his Michigan State teammate Kirk Ziemke about an experience Kirk had during his freshman year on the team.

"Labor Day weekend in my freshman year, I had been off from school for a week. I was 17 years old then, and a little bit younger than I am now. I came back to my room from dinner and we are getting ready to go out and there was a message on my answering machine. When I checked to see who the message was from and played the message I heard: 'This is Dr. Clarence Underwood, I'm the athletic director at

Michigan State University. I would like to talk to you. We've uncovered some things about where you worked at this summer and it really doesn't please me since we are now unsure about your eligibility. Please call me right away.' At about this point I almost passed out after hearing this and I thought to myself 'Oh my God what did I do?' and again I'm thinking what did I do over the summer, didn't I pay taxes or what? So I was nervous and so I looked in the phonebook and looked up Dr. Underwood's number and I called his office and got his answering machine and left a message. I did not know what was going on. I was very nervous and shaking. I was thinking 'What's my dad going to say? Who can I call?' Our first practice was Monday, and I was really nervous. So I got the phonebook and looked up Dr. Underwood's home telephone number. I called and his wife answered. I explained the situation and she said: "Oh he's not home." So I asked her, 'Do you know where he is?' She tells me that he is in Oregon for the MSU football game. At that moment I was thinking 'Oh my God, he's calling from Oregon, this must be the worst possible thing'. ... I'm thinking I will be thrown out of school and be back working in the factory.... I am really nervous and upset at this point. My roommate convinces me to go out and relax a little bit and to go over to John's house on Marigold Street. The whole time we were walking over there I am thinking 'Oh God, you know, my student and swimming career is over'. Finally we get there, and I'm standing in the kitchen, and just thinking, I'm worrying, and I hear Munley talking in the corner, and I was like thinking 'that voice sounds so familiar'. So I hear him talking, and it just dawns on me, it was like that's the voice of Dr. Underwood on the answering machine. I went over to talk to John and I asked him 'Did you leave a message on my machine?' And he was like, "oh yeah did you get that?" And I am like 'Did I get it? I called Dr. Underwood's office and left a message, I called his home, and I ended up giving his wife my home number and I am going home for the weekend.' I went home for the weekend and Sunday morning I wake up and it was about

8:30 in the morning. My dad says, you got a phone call from Dr. Underwood. I was like uh-oh, oh my God what am I going to tell him? I'm afraid he's going to ask me, how did you get into this school? I was afraid he was going to go over and see my transcripts. So he called and he's like 'yeah, my wife called me in Oregon and told me you had some questions and said I left a message on your answering machine?' I was like, awe, yeah, well I kind of got tricked by another teammate. He left the message and I'm sorry for disturbing you and your wife. Dr. Underwood replied: 'Oh, this is just the first week of school, looks like you are going to have a long year.'"

John was blessed with wonderful friends. He knew how to have fun, how to enjoy himself, how to live life to the fullest. He brought much joy and happiness to his family and to his friends.

Highlights in Pictures

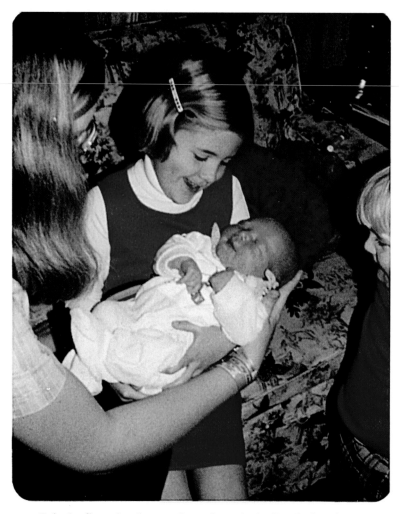

John's first day home from hospital after being born
with Mom, Elizabeth and Michael

John swimming with a kick board at a very early age.

John catching a fish in the pond behind our home with brothers Thomas and Michael.

John on the starting block at swim practice at
Portage West Middle School.

John feeding Quackers and friends behind home.

John sledding in the backyard with his swim goggles
to keep the snow out of his eyes.

John's idea for a stupid human trick for the
David Letterman Show- outside in the snow in a swim suit.

John, Michael, Thomas and Coach Schafer at a Portage
Central High School Swim Meet.

Munley family getting ready for a group photo in the
backyard. Mom and Katie are trying to keep John in line.
Note future in-law Doug on the far right of the line-up.

John receiving his Portage Central High School Diploma

Katie, John, Liz, Tom, and Mike at Liz's Graduation at
Michigan State University.

John, Katie and Elizabeth

John and Coach Gianiodis discussing swim strategy.

Swimming freestyle

John's 500 yard freestyle finish at Big Ten Championships.

John receiving Big Ten Championship Plaque
from University of Michigan Coach Jon Urbanchek.

John and Pat at Big Ten Championships.

John surfing in Hawaii

Doug, Liz, Katie, Thomas, Stephanie, Michael, John,
Mary Anne and Pat

Chapter 3

April 30, 2001

Monday morning, April 30th 2001 was a beautiful morning, with not a cloud in the pure blue sky. When I saw the sky that morning I remembered that someone once told me that Ernest Hemingway wrote about the Michigan skies on days like the 30th. I decided to go on a run, ran for about 3 miles, and went into work at the University. About 1:00 in the afternoon the phone rang and Coach G, Matt Gianiodis the assistant swim coach from Michigan State was on the line and asked if Coach Bader had talked to me. I said no. He said there was a problem with John and I needed to call Coach Bader right away and he gave me a number to call. I asked him what was the problem and Coach G said something to the effect that he wasn't sure but I needed to call Coach Bader right away. I called the number and Coach Bader answered. I told him Coach G had reached me and asked me to call him about John. "He asked you to call me?" he said surprised and I said, "What is the problem with John?" He asked me to wait a minute and then another man came on the phone and introduced himself as a police officer and asked me if I was John's father. I said, "What is wrong with John? As dreadful images began to pass through my mind, scenes of auto accidents, people hurt, something terrible being wrong. The officer said, "Are you sitting down?" I said emphatically "Tell me what is wrong with John, what has happened?" At that point he said, "John is dead". Stunned I said, "John is dead. John can't be dead, what are you telling me? He said again "John is dead." "He collapsed while jogging on Harrison Road." I replied, "Was there an accident? Was he hit by a car? "Was he hit by someone on his bike?" The officer said, "No, it was witnessed, he was jogging, he stopped and took off his shirt as if hot, and then collapsed. The EMT's were called and arrived right away, he was taken to the hospital but he died." After a pause the officer then said "I am sorry we didn't reach you sooner but he had no identification on him. He was just wearing his running shorts and shirt." I responded "Well maybe it's not John, it can't be John, this cannot have happened." The officer asked: "Does your son have a tattoo of a frog on one hip? And before I could answer he said: "And a Spartan S on the other?" His words and the images they communicated swiftly cut like a sharp sword through the remaining denial and left no doubt and I simply said: "That's John."

After receiving the call I left the University to go and tell Mary Anne. I didn't say anything to anyone at the University because somehow it seemed that John's mother should know what happened before anyone else. I drove to her school in Comstock, Michigan still dazed from the news, and went directly to the superintendent's office, which was next door, and asked the superintendent to accompany me to Mary Anne's classroom. I had some terrible news to tell her and she would have to leave class. He asked me what had happened and I said that I just couldn't talk about it until I talked to her. We walked to her classroom together and as soon as she saw us she started to cry and asked what was wrong, what had happened. I told her. She collapsed on the floor in tears and had to be helped upstairs. We then had the impossible task of calling John's brothers and sisters. You should never have to tell someone over the phone that their son, brother or sister, or any loved one has died suddenly. However, there was no choice. They had to know and know immediately. I reached Thomas in Grand Rapids, Elizabeth's husband, Doug, in East Lansing, Michael in Chicago and Katie in Tempe, Arizona. Since Katie was all by herself so far from Michigan we first called a priest on the campus of Arizona State University who went to her room and was there when we called. I will never forget her sobbing on the phone and saying over and over that it could not be "Our

John". Were they sure it was our John? I didn't have the heart to tell her that I was sure it was John because of his tattoos. I just told her they were very sure but we were going up to the hospital to see him.

We then drove to Lansing to the hospital and met Thomas and Elizabeth there. We talked to the doctor who treated John when he was brought in to the ER. She said that he was experiencing an arrhythmia when the EMTs arrived on the scene and the type of rhythm he was in was a precursor to his going into full arrest. They tried to shock him back into a normal heart rhythm but were unsuccessful. She said they did everything they could but she felt he was probably gone before he arrived at the ER. An autopsy would be done the next day. After talking to the doctor we were escorted to the morgue.

We had to wait several agonizing minutes while the staff prepared for us to see John. We were taken into a small room with a glass window. While we expected to be in the same room with John we were not allowed to be in the room with him. When I told the nurse we would like to go into the room to be with John she said that was not possible. Since his death was unexpected and considered a coroner's case, we were not allowed to be with John. The nurse commented 'young people just do not die suddenly like this. I suddenly recalled a story I had seen on CBS's 60 minutes some years before. The story discussed how intelligence agencies assassinated people out in the open in the full view of the public. According to the story agents used an umbrella with a hidden needle at the tip that could surreptitiously inject a drug into an unsuspecting victim walking along the street causing an instantaneous heart attack. I wondered to myself: Are you implying that something like this happened to John? I knew this was a crazy thought but that's what came to mind as soon as she made her comment. While we wanted to be in the room with John, for the moment we could only look at John through the window glass, touch our hands to the window in his direction and cry.

The next morning I called the forensic pathologist who was scheduled to do John's autopsy, Dr. Joyce de Jong. I introduced myself and told her we were desperate to know as soon as possible what had happened to John because his sudden death was incomprehensible and had devastated the family. She was very kind and listened, took some time and asked some questions about John's medical history, and then told me that she was going to perform the autopsy later that morning. She estimated how long the procedure would take and informed me she would call me as soon as the procedure was over to let me know the preliminary findings.

When she called back after the autopsy was completed she said that all she could determine was that John had an enlarged heart. She indicated that an enlarged heart was not necessarily unusual among athletes and it was not clear how much of a role the enlarged heart played in his sudden death. She indicated that she would have to wait for the results of the final toxicology testing; however, the preliminary indications, later confirmed by all toxicology testing results being negative, were that drugs or medications did not play any role, and his sudden death appeared to be due to Cardiac Arrhythmia. After discussing her preliminary findings she asked permission to send the electrical conduction system of John's heart to researchers at Walter Reed Hospital in Washington, D.C. These investigators were studying sudden and unexpected death and she felt that further study of this type at Walter Reed might yield more information. I said yes, we wanted to know as much as we could about what had happened.

Weeks later we were to be told that the doctors at Walter Reed concluded that there were two factors in John's death: an enlarged heart and small vessel dysplasia or thickening near the AV node of the heart. The AV node is a kind of electrical relay station in the heart and this type of small vessel thickening in this system of the heart had been found by the researchers to be associated with sudden death.

Shortly after talking to the doctor on Tuesday I talked to John's current head coach, Coach Lutz and told him the preliminary findings of the autopsy on John so he and John's teammates would have some idea as to what happened. The need to make some sense out of this and to find out what had happened was tremendous. Shortly after our phone call the coach was in a press conference and shared the preliminary findings, which appeared in the newspapers the next day. I didn't intend for this to happen. John's sister, Katie was still in Arizona and was not going to be home from Arizona until later the next day. I wanted to tell her the findings in person before she could see it in the papers or hear the news from someone else while flying home from Arizona.

Next Mary Anne and I had to select a cemetery plot for John. We went to the Texas Township Town Hall and met with the clerk in charge of cemetery plots. Residents of Texas Township are eligible for a free cemetery plot in Hope Cemetery, one of the Township's Cemeteries. While the funeral home director offered to make the arrangements I needed to see where John would be buried. Hope Cemetery was within a mile of our home so it seemed like a good choice. I had driven by the cemetery innumerable times but I had never really noticed it. I had a vague recollection of Katie telling me that she and her good friend Megan were out that way one day riding bikes and had stopped at the cemetery to read the names and dates on the headstones and telling me about some of the very old dates that were on the markers dating back over 100 years.

The township clerk met with us and showed us a map of the cemetery and what plots were available. We went out to the cemetery and walked around and picked out three plots together, one for John and one for Mary Anne and one for me. We selected plots in a newer section of the cemetery where there were a number of young people recently buried. Somehow this seemed appropriate. Right near where John would be there was a young man, Michael Steven Hizer, who ran track in high school and died at the young age of 27.

Nearby also rests Jonathan Abraham Stryd, a young man who died at age 24. Young people we never knew but names we see every time we go to the cemetery.

That evening I went out to get the evening newspaper and was stunned to see John's picture on the front page of the Kalamazoo Gazette with the story of his death. The paper had interviewed John's high school swim coach, Jim Schafer, and they had done a very nice story about John. Coach Schafer's words were very comforting. He said that John got the most out of his God-given ability; more than any other swimmer he had known, John wanted to be the best he could be. However, the sight of John's picture on the front page of the paper in association with his death was just too much to bear. There would be other stories about John in the Gazette as well as articles about John in the Lansing State Journal and the MSU State News. I tried to stay away from all the newspaper stories about John for weeks and months thereafter.

As difficult as it was to even think clearly, to function and do simple things, we somehow managed to plan the memorial and church service for John, one that we hoped would show John how much we loved and cared for him. There were two days of visitation, followed by a reflection service Friday evening and the funeral Mass on Saturday morning. John's brothers and sisters made a CD of music that reminded them of John to play during the visitation because whenever John had gone to visitations he always complained about the music as being too somber. His brothers and sisters selected John's pictures, awards and recognition displayed during the visitations. Elizabeth and Michael gave eulogies during the reflection service Friday evening and Thomas, Katie and I gave eulogies during the funeral Mass on Saturday. From his home in East Lansing Thomas brought Winston to the funeral home to be next to John's casket in the funeral home during the visitation.

Chapter 4

Reflections

The following are the eulogies presented at John's reflection service Friday evening and during his funeral mass on Saturday morning.

My Brother John the CHAMPION

by his big sister Liz

About 9 months before John was born, God was working on his recruiting for the Munley Team. He was looking for an individual who could be a **CHAMPION**... not just in athletics, but in life. John decided this team would be a good fit for him because he could add qualities that our team was missing and complement those already on the team.

On April 11, as mom and dad were at Dr. Munro's office in Denville, New Jersey, for a typical check up. Dr. Munro said, "Pat and Mary Anne go to the hospital."

Dad said, "Well, do I have time to get something to eat? I wasn't planning on the baby being born today." As Pat & Mary Anne left the doctor's office and drove through Burger King, John was getting his pep talk about the big race he had ahead of him. His coach for life reminded him of the strategy they had discussed earlier. John never had a doubt in his ability to handle the role.

At 11:43 pm, the gun went off and John dove into the world.

As he went through the race he was a **C**omedian. As a comedian, some of his favorite shows were Cheers, Night Court, and Seinfeld. Just yesterday, I said to my family, it is so hard to believe that our family clown who made us all laugh so much, is why we are here to shed our tears of pain as opposed to tears of laughter. So for a moment let's transform those tears of pain into tears of laughter. Over the past few days I have heard so many stories I never heard before, each one of them different, each one with laughter. Think of your own John story that makes your heart laugh. As you think about that, listen to these "deep thoughts" by JPM.

- Favorite words – "Tuna. Because if you spell it backwards you get A NUT. And I see myself as kind of a crazy person."

- Favorite figure of speech – " 'what a fox' It's not my favorite but I think it's funny, good looking people get compared to an animal that eats small rodents and eats chickens. I think it's more of an insult. And when I say to people "you're a fox" then they think that they're cool. I just laugh."

- Favorite metaphor – "Life's a bitch" – I'll let you tell me.

- Favorite simile – " 'My mistress' eyes are nothing like the sun' You got to give William Shakespeare credit. He sits there rippin' on his girl friend yet turns it into a compliment. His Sonnet 130 was revolutionary to me."

John was a **HERO** to many both young and old. He was a role model to kids like young Mitchell Jump who loved it when John came home from MSU to play legos and the child whose name is unknown because he doesn't know John personally, but aspires to be like him because of all his swimming accomplishments. He was also a hero to those old

37

like his Papa Ed, who still can't believe his grandson John qualified and participated in the Olympic Trials.

John was an **A**ccomplished Athlete. The fact that John was not heavily recruited out of high school and went on to be the Most Valuable Swimmer, four years in a row, and finished his senior season with a school record, shows his work ethic and determination. The fact John died while running, is just all too ironic.

John was a **M**unley. Grandson of Edward Munley, Son of Patrick & Mary Anne Munley, and brother to Elizabeth, Thomas, Michael, and Katie Munley. A young man very proud of his Irish heritage.

John was a **P**artier. While John may not have always been the life of the party he certainly thought life was a party and never passed up an opportunity to have fun with friends or family. Whether it was at Thomas' house, at the Marriott with Fred, tailgating at Breslin, or at the Evergreen with Dave... John was going to be there and having fun. At friends' houses, when the song "Wishlist" by Pearl Jam came on John made everyone sing along. Make sure the next time you hear the song, you sing along because John is watching.

John was **I**ntellectual. I'm sure you're wondering how I'm going to justify John being intellectual, especially his chemistry teacher. I mean after all, he didn't exactly show the same work ethic in the classroom as he did in the pool. But I really do think that John was intellectual. Right after John returned home from Hawaii, we went out for dinner and I asked John about his trip. Seeing as he was a 21 year old college student I expected him to be telling me about the babes, the sun and the surf. However, he surprised me and talked about going to Pearl Harbor and seeing the Memorial and hiking up a volcano with friends. I was just shocked to hear this. However, I truly believe that when John was with us and sitting there quietly, he was taking notes, constantly thinking, and taking lessons from life.

John was **O**pinionated. John was always quick to share his opinion. He did it in a very direct way and never sugar coated anything. He was what one may call brutally honest. However, these days we can only appreciate honesty. He didn't expect you to agree with him, but would tell you his opinion. I can only wonder what his opinion is of all of this.

John loved **N**ature. The lake at Rock Spring, the tree by the sand box, minnows, gold fish, snow, the pond in our backyard, fishing, canoeing, dirt trails, ducks and the sand hill are all things in nature John loved. The beautiful summer- like days we have recently had, should only remind us to stop and take in the beautiful world we live in… just as John did.

On April 30, 2001 at 11:38 John crossed under the flags heading towards heaven. He slowed down and hit the touch pad hard at 12:10 I only hope he had the same image as he does on the cards you all have today, very pleased with his performance. I know we are all pleased with the life he just finished!

"Good life John, we'll see you in heaven."

Elizabeth Peot
May 4, 2001

An Older Brother Remembers

Over the past few days I've been racking my brain for my best memories with John—just the two of us. Trying to find the right anecdote that features John's "wit."

But I've found that the stories that have stuck in my mind are ones where words aren't important...and I think that's because we managed to get along well without too many words.

I remember a time when we were young—elementary aged or so—and took a canoe ride down the stream, for either a frog hunt or a pleasure cruise. We went down to a side pond—which I think John had discovered for the family as the best place for frog hunting—spent some time down there, and then went back on our way home.

On the way back, we both looked over the right side of the canoe at something—maybe a big fish—and lost our balance...then we both leaned to the left and simultaneously realizing our mistake overcorrected to the right side...and the boat tipped over. After I found my soft footing on the bottom of the creek and finished sputtering out the nasty, algae filled water from my mouth, I looked for John. I soon found him staring back at me, a little bewildered, a little bemused. We just kind of shook our heads, like "this sucks," and then set about the tedious tasks of gathering our floating gear, righting the canoe and getting it over to land so we could drain it.

But that was from the peaceful half of our relationship. Much of the time, John had a great fight—physical and otherwise—on his brain, and I feel like it was often directed at me.

On one of the physical fight occasions, John decided after school one day that I was going to give him a piggyback ride, and he jumped on my back. At first, I tried gently to peel him off of me, but that didn't work. So then I tried a less gentle bucking bronco defense. This worked.

But, as John fell off of me, he landed awkwardly on his feet, stumbled backwards, tripped over the dog, fell, and hit his head on the runner of a wooden rocking chair.

Annoyed from the incident, I was slow to react to the crash behind me, but I soon found John bleeding from the back of his head. I spent time trying to stop the flow of blood from his head with a mass of paper towels over the kitchen sink. And as I'm doing this, John is asking me with both concern and scientific curiosity: "Can you see my brain? Can you see my skull?"

As much as I was concerned about John, I kept fearing more my father's reaction, which was right-in-line with what I was expecting. After John went to the doctor and got stitches, my dad called me up to his room. "Michael," he said, "you need to stop picking on your little brother, you could have killed him today."

"But Dad," I protested, "John attacked me!"

"Well, whatever. You two are brothers and you shouldn't be fighting."

Dad just didn't get the fight that was in John.

As we grew older, John focused his fights from the directly physical, to the more esoteric ones in the swimming pool. My senior year in high school, and John's sophomore year, I began to feel threatened by John in the water.

Now, I've always placed greatest emphasis on where you stood at the end of the season, but midway through the season, John was consistently a couple of seconds faster than me in the 200 freestyle.

It became pretty distressing for me, to say the least. I was the older brother—I was supposed to be faster. I kept thinking of Jim Schafer's theory that the youngest is always the best in a family of swimmers. I was ready to accept that John would be a better swimmer than me, but it absolutely had to wait until after I had left Central.

So, coming into the conference meet, the last meet of the season if you don't make the state meet, I felt the pressure building. I didn't shave for prelims: the point of my prelim swim was just to qualify for the finals. I slothed around for 200 yards on Friday and qualified 5th, John qualified 2nd, and Chris Bradford, my young nemesis from the previous season, was 1st.

Shaving that night, my goal was clear: BEAT JOHN. Not defend my conference championship in the 200 from the previous year, but just BEAT JOHN.

And I'm sure John had a similar goal: BEAT MICHAEL. I mean, he was so badly looking for an extra second to drop that he shaved his eyebrows.

Saturday afternoon, we dove into the water for the 200. I kept trying to peak over from lane 1 to the middle lanes where John was. My first 50, I felt awesome. I was in that zone, where you've just shaved and you can feel the water shooting past you and know that your personal bests are about to fall by the wayside. But when I flipped at the 50 mark, I found that I was a good second behind John.

I was frustrated, but not deterred. A mantra played in my head: BEAT JOHN, BEAT JOHN, BEAT JOHN; and that provided the rhythm for my long, strong strokes.

As I approached the wall to finish, I had no idea where I stood in the race. But it was time for the championship finish, just like the ones Jim made us do in practice regularly— during which John and the rest of us always would goof off and finish with a fist pump or V-shaped arms.

I knew that day there would be no fist pump championship finish for me, just a quick glance to the scoreboard. And when I looked at the clock, I found that not only did I triumph over John, but I had also won the race.

I looked over to John and he just had that bemused look on his face, with dashes of confusion, surprise, and pride.

I hope that you don't think that the point of this story is for me to relive my besting my younger brother one more time. Instead, this story reminds me how much John pushed me to my limits. I'm convinced today that if I hadn't been racing John and having him push me, I probably would have ended my high school swimming career shut-out from an individual conference championship.

I'm truly glad though, that that wasn't our last race together. A week later, we swam together on a 400 free relay, and broke a varsity record that had been older than both of us.

I mentioned before that John and I shared a certain wordless communication, but what has pained me most over the past few days is that in our silence, I left unsaid so many things I should have said to him.

I always imagined us sharing this combination Hall-mark-Old Milwaukee-"it doesn't get any better than this" moment, where I tell John what he's meant to me.

"John" I'd say, "I never thought that the smelly, messy, family clown would give me so much in my life. Not only did you teach me silly things like where to catch the best frogs, how to wire up a Nintendo or Sega, but you became an example of how hard work and dedication can lead to anything. I remember being at work and watching the real-time results for the Olympic Trials on the Internet, and although it defied every logical and rational thought I had, I truly believed that somehow you would qualify to go to Sydney. Because, you'd come so far in life that it just became too hard to believe that you wouldn't make it happen. John, I'm proud of the man you've become. Thanks for being here to make me a better person."

Michael Patrick Munley

May 4, 2001

John Patrick Munley

This past weekend the Gospel was about how the apostles had gone out fishing and on their way back they see a man standing on shore. At first they do not recognize that it is Jesus, but eventually they do, and they tell him that they had not caught anything. He told them to cast their net over to the right. When they tried to pull the net up they couldn't because there were so many fish. 100 and 53 to be exact. This was a very significant number in the Bible because that's how many different types of fish they believed were in Mediterranean at the time.

I found it very interesting that the Gospel of the week that John went up to heaven should involve Jesus telling other people how to fish. Upon John's arrival in heaven I can just see it now, John's first conversation with Jesus, "That's nice JC, but what do you know about catching frogs?" That is John. Only John could challenge the Son of God when it came to things dealing with the water. John is my older brother who is the closest to me in age.

So here we are at John's funeral. Wow, things you thought you would never say or want to say, that ranks right up there.

Whenever anyone dies, it's a very sad time. Those words only underestimate the incomprehensible nature of these events. But you know there have already been enough tears. It is time to focus on John's life and as it says in what my parents call, the brochure, this is a celebration of life. So let's celebrate John's life.

One of the things John likes to do is watch television. One of his favorite shows is Seinfeld. When someone asked Jerry Seinfeld, aren't you sad about your show being over? He replied, "Why should I be so sad about something that was so good?" And that's how we need to look at John's life. But the fact is that we are sad, we are hurting and we are in pain. Whenever something like this happens, it is so easy to ask why? Why God? Why him? We know that John has a good life, is very blessed, he touches all of our lives, he makes us laugh and for some of us he made us cry when he was alive. Yea for John beating me up as an older brother.

We ask why, because we know all of the other wonderful memories, he has yet to live. Knowing this, we need to ask why in a different respect. We need to ask why, when we wake up in the morning. We have to ask ourselves why, when we have the ability to open our mouths and sound comes out forming words and sentences. We need to ask ourselves why, when God gives us two feet to walk on, two ears to hear with, two eyes to see with, and two hands to touch the works of art that he has created for us. We need to ask ourselves why God has given us the gifts he has. Which leads us to the second question that we need to ask ourselves. What? What is it that God wants us to do, and then and only then can we answer the first question.

When we look at someone like John who has so much going for him. He is a genuine human being, has a wonderful sense of humor, gives everything he has into what he does. When we look at someone like John whose's life ended too soon, our first reaction may be that life is too short and that you should live each day like it's your last, but I disagree. We need to live each day like it's our first. The first time we feel the breeze stand up every hair on our face. The first time we feel the sun warm our backs. The first time the waves lap against our legs. The first time you look into a child eyes; the miracle of their existence and know God exists and only then can we truly be grateful for life. I once heard that, if the only prayer you ever say is thank you that will be enough.

I also remember something that John always used to say to me, "shut up." Come on he was my older brother, he didn't walk on water; he swam through it. Perhaps I have really just been delaying the inevitable part of his eulogy with these motivational reflections. So on with John. Even though in school John's majoring in packaging, he also

45

practiced a little bit of philosophy. John once said, "The sharpest crayon is the one still in the box." Thanks John. That is John. The honest, blunt, hard working John, who never sugar coats anything. In our sometimes-superficial society it is so easy to create this mask to the world. John had no mask. You always know that you are getting the God's honest truth and you know that you can trust him. John also has incredible integrity and character. Someone said, " lead by example and if necessary use words." That statement epitomizes John Munley.

Actually I have come to the conclusion that everything important in life, I learned from John in our backyard. We grew up on a pond, then there is a land bridge, and a stream with a hidden pond attached at the end.

The three main lessons that I've learned from John are; patience, caring and perseverance. When we were younger, Michael, John and I used to catch frogs and turtles; mainly it was just two of us at a time. John was always involved in the process. When we would be in the hidden pond John would sit there for 10 or 15 minutes in the canoe waiting to catch a frog. And if I flinched, ...well let me back up. John also followed our dad in psychology; in that John is a big believer in behavior modification. If I whispered "John I don't..." and before anything else came out, watch out because there was a paddle chucking water right at me. "Shut-up, don't talk!" I loved watching him, I know that he is good at what he does. Before I was wet what I was trying to ask was, "John I don't see what you're looking at." Years passed before I could ever get up to his skill, truly he never worked on it, it was always just there, *and he* always looked deeper. The second thing that John teaches me is caring. A couple of years ago, many I guess, the dam broke at the end of the stream and it was beginning to dry up in places and fish along with other creatures were beginning to die. Well, one night I remember very distinctively John wanted me to come down there with him. It was late in the evening too, so we took a flashlight. He told me that earlier in the day he had been taking fish from the stream and putting them in the pond. So they would live. "Can I do it, John?" "Yes. Pick up the fish with two hands and go put it in the pond. O.k.? It's not that hard." We were probably down there for at least an hour maybe longer. One fish I put in the pond it just stayed there. I pointed at it and said, "This one didn't live." He said, " Not all of them do. Come back over here and get more." I felt good. Empowered. John showed me the importance of caring about every life form.

John also taught me lessons in perseverance. My favorite is in the winter, when we would make a path for our sleds and when we would get to the end, I'd try to get up and he would push me down. I'd try to stand up again and he pushed me back down again. I said, "John!" " What's the matter Katie? What's the matter? Having a little trouble getting up?" As I kept trying to stand up he pushed me back down. I laughed. No one can make me laugh like John can.

Can is a very powerful word. John knows he can. He always believes in himself. I once read in God's Little Character Instruction Book, "When God measures a man, he puts the tape around the heart, not the brain." If even medical records find his heart to be off the charts, you know he is amazing in God's eyes.

One of the things John is known for, is his swimming accomplishments. These must be kept in proper perspective. He has skills, gifts and focus that others can only dream of. His achievements are evidence of his hard work, dedication, and un-selfishness. Truly- outstanding. The reality is records are broken, awards will tarnish, lists will be edited, and more athletes awake in the dawn tomorrow. None like John, he is unique. The perspective is as people we can't list the last ten Heisman trophy winners, Miss Americas, or Nobel Prize winners. However, we can list ten people who have touched our lives, taught us lessons and who we love, and those are the only lists that are important.

As siblings, friends or in many of your cases especially parents, we need to remember to be proud of our children no matter what they do. As we list his accolades and accomplishments it is imperative that we remember for future generations that we are equally as proud of John and our children even if he had never or they never step foot onto a field, into the arena or on the pool deck, because they have stepped into our hearts.

We are proud of John because he is our brother, he is our son, he is our grandson, he is our nephew, he is our godchild, but last and most important he is our friend. John is a brother to two brothers Thomas and Michael, and two sisters Elizabeth and myself. Once there was five. And that has not changed. There will always be five.

And John, even when we're looking up at you in heaven, know that nothing has changed, because we have been looking up to you all along. But John honestly, when you're teaching JC how to catch frogs I know the splashing worked for me, but I might advise against it with Jesus. John, there are three words which made me smile. I emailed you about your internship with Philip Morris confirming that you would be packaging more than just cigarettes. And you replied back, "actually just cigarettes." Well now, I have three words for you "I love you." You change my life. You change others' lives. John, as I grew up with you, I observed your wisdom and now I'll take advantage of the advice you've been giving me all along. I'm going to shut up now. You take care of yourself, everyone loves you, thank you and you let me know if you catch anything.

Katherine Claire Munley

May 5, 2001

John Patrick Munley
The First Without...

A good friend of mine called as I was writing this, and I told him that this was hard. This whole experience is, without question, the hardest thing I have ever been through. He told me to speak from the heart. And he said that he and his wife were thinking of my family. I thought to myself, I would love to speak from my heart, but my heart is broken.

Freshmen Year: The Spartans will also look to freshman John Munley, an untapped talent who shows tremendous promise in a variety of races from the 50 to the mile..... "Depending on his maturing process over the next four years, he has the potential to be one of the best swimmers Michigan State has ever had," Bader said.

When I was 13, our family had a beautiful golden retriever, with a short blond coat and legs longer than any I'd seen. Getting the dog was the result of a carefully negotiated deal between myself and my parents for some swimming accomplishment. While technically the dog was mine, everyone loved her, and played with her. She was this beautiful puppy that had grown very tall over the 8 months we had her. One day I was in the middle of practice during Christmas vacation and my sister Elizabeth walked in. Not all that uncommon, but I noticed the look on her face and knew something was wrong. And all she said was that Medley had collapsed while playing and that I needed to come right away. This wonderful creature who we loved, and who loved us had died. The veterinarian mentioned something about it being a congenital heart defect and offered sympathies. I really did not care why, I just knew that something I loved dearly was gone, for no good reason, and it did not feel good. While the similarities are striking, I am not going to compare my brother to our once beloved family pet.

The great thing about my parents is that they were not about to let this happen. No, sir. Not during Christmas. On Christmas Eve, my father would take me to a breeder and we would go get another dog. Another golden puppy, who immediately made all of us happy, who filled the void that was created. It was exactly what the doctor ordered. This dog lived up until last Saturday when John, my mother, and I had to make the decision to euthanize her and put her out of her misery. As the vet began to euthanize her, my mother and I continued to pet her as she stopped breathing, but for some reason John did not. He watched and said nothing.

At the time I thought why isn't he saying good-bye to this dog that has shared 13 years with us. I wanted to tell him, politely, to get his butt over here and pet this dog good-bye, but I did not. I just accepted that this was a side of John that I did not understand. Just as we are all here trying to understand why John is now gone, I can tell you that all I want to do is to go to the great brother tree and just pick another one. If such a tree existed, we might be able to find something close to John, but we could never replace him. And the void that has been created in our lives, would not be filled. While we all had things that we did not understand about John, I can tell you what we did.

Sophomore Year: Sophomore John Munley also returns full force to lead MSU in the freestyle events. "Our real standout has to be John Munley," Bader said.

We all understood that John was his own person. If he was doing something out of the ordinary, there was always a reason for it. At least he thought it was a reason. To be honest, often times we really had to ask ourselves what those reasons may be. John did things in his own way, with his own style, in his own time. The nickname he had written on his pull bouy was "MUNSTAR" And like a star, John burned so very bright, before burning out. And now we are left with what feels like a black hole. The absence of John is a powerful force.

On the outside John lived each day like he was at Disney World. Whether he was playing video games or Frisbee golf, watching 50 channels on TV simultaneously, taking the batteries out of the remote control for the TV and leaving the channel set to PBS, assisting John Breusch, our roommate, with the building of a snow fort. Because, as John put it, "It's not like we want a snow fort, We NEED a snow fort." John lived like the meaning of the words, Carpe Diem.

On the inside, John always had the right idea in the back of his head. There was the time he went out to shovel our retired neighbor's driveway during the blizzard last December. When our neighbor offered to pay him, he said no thank you, I'm going to Hawaii. The time he went to talk to Coach Lutz and got a former teammate re-instated after he was done swimming. Or even just last weekend, as John gave tips to my parent's 5 year-old neighbor on how to catch the most frogs. The best practice, according to John, a large net. John just knew what was right.

Junior Year "Those swimmers that make trials are usually going to be your leaders," Bader said. "John Munley is definitely our power man in the water"

My brother was not a saint, at least not yet. If he takes that same charismatic grin and asks God to see what he can do about a little sainthood, he may just get it. He certainly knew how to push the envelope. Whether he was taking my Jeep because he had no money to go fill his car with gas, or whether he was leaving countless dishes and glasses un-cleaned in the sink, or responding to a statement of what you thought with "Oh, Do You?!" In the end, I would match his smile with one of my own, fill the Jeep with gas after he used it, and cleaned his dishes for him. Occasionally I would sarcastically ask him if this bothered him. And with a dry smile, and his trademark cautious indifference, John would reply "I know you're going to do it sooner or later so why bother." I would just roll my eyes and think to myself, that's John. This ability of his to charm his way through anything, was a quintessential part of why we loved him. John, you are really pushing it this time, and I am really not happy about it.

Everyone has said if there is anything I can do, please let me know. And every time we say thank you, and that, unfortunately there is nothing to do. I have considered this question long and hard over the past few days, and I can now tell you all what you can do. As we face this First year Without John, keep him in your hearts and thoughts.

On this First Saturday Without John, I would like to share a few thoughts as to when you may pause to think of him.

To my family,

Mom, the First time you come to East Lansing Without a care package for John,

Dad the First time you call Without the need to ask me to make sure my brother's head is screwed on straight,

Elizabeth, the First time you call Without inviting John out to dinner with you and Doug,

Michael, the First time we are all home for Easter, Memorial Day, or Festivus and we play home run derby or football Without John,

Katie, the First time you go into the backyard, Without John being there to teach you a lesson in life,

Papa Ed, the First time you write those checks for Christmas, and write them Without one for John,

Aunt Diana, the First time you tell Papa Ed how all of Pat's children are doing Without mentioning John,

Sister Jeremiah, the First time you call out to Kalamazoo, Without talking to John,

To John's Friends,

Little Guy, the First time you have a party Without any memorable behavior from my brother John,

John Breusch, the First Sunday dinner at 1061 Glenhaven Without John,

Joe, the First time you go back to Crunchy's for a bucket Without John,

Kirk, the First time you go to your locker after practice and find it Without a picture left by John,

Alex, the First time you go to practice Without John, remember why it is you can go to practice,

Dippy, the First time you sit down to play Play-station Without John,

Dave and Mark, the First double cheeseburgers from McDonald's Without John,

Tings, the First time you go to Sparty's Without John,

Fred, the First GBS, Without John,

Adam, the First round of frisbee golf Without John,

Ildiko, Brooke, and Stephanie, the First time someone asks who you dated in college Without knowing that one of those people is gone,

The Michigan State Swim Team, the First time you enter into a battle in the shade Without John, take some of his confidence and a little more of his heart with you,

To the Michigan State Swimming Alumni and Friends, the First alumni meet Without John,

Jim Schafer, the First time someone asks about one of those old guys on the record board, don't tell a story Without speaking of John,

To those of you with brothers, the First time you see your brother after this, tell him you love him Without hesitation,

To those of you with sons, the First time you look at your son, think of what your life would be like Without him and thank God that you have him with you,

Senior Year: The First year Without a Media Guide for me to shamelessly steal a quote.

At Michigan State we have a tradition called the Golden Spike. It is given to those seniors who are at the end of their swimming careers. Mine hangs right behind the TV in my house. Last Tuesday I came home from work and noticed that where there had been one Golden Spike, there were now two. John had hung his on the same nail with mine. I smiled and stopped to read the poem that is attached to it. It is a poem written by one of two brothers who swam at Michigan State, in the 40's and 50's. And I thought of the countless Alumni Meets that Jack and Dave Seibold have attended together. And, I thought, in six short months John and I will go to our first Alumni meet together, as members of the same team. John and I both swam for a long time, but not once were we members on the same team. We were five years apart. I had always longed for the time when I could step behind the blocks for a relay, look into his eyes, him looking into mine, both of us knowing that the other was not going to let him down. The poem on the Golden Spike, titled "Hang it Up", concludes with, "Tis time Old veteran, hang it up, hang it up."

John, I will hang it up, and finish my thoughts with these two;

John, you are the First to be Without the uncertainty of what lies beyond this world.

And John, you are the First person that I do not want to live Without.

We love you, John.

Thomas Edward Munley

May 5, 2001

John Patrick Munley

Someone once told me that Ernest Hemingway used to write about the skies in Michigan and how on certain days when you look up and take notice there is not a single cloud in the sky and the sky is perfectly blue – Monday morning April 30 was one of those days Hemingway described– a perfectly clear blue sky – a day full of sunshine – a day when you just feel just great to be alive and to be out in the sun, - and when I got up on Monday and looked out I said to myself this is a Hemingway day - a day too good to miss just by going right to work - I really need to go out and jog before work to really enjoy the day. So I ran from about 9 to 9:30, showered, felt great and went on to the University. Apparently, about two hours later that same morning John decided to do the same thing, maybe like father like son, go out for a jog on that beautiful morning –Monday April 30th really was a great day for a run – a great day to be alive.

After hearing about John I was devastated beyond words – the deepest pain I have ever felt, I don't think I can ever remember feeling so bad as I did when I received the call about John – on such a beautiful day how could John be dead – how could I be alive – if anyone was to have had to die on a run this morning surely it should have been me, 53 years old not John at age 22 – how was this possible. This was not right, not fair, you don't take the younger player out of the game before the older one, life was not playing by the rules, this was out of bounds, a flagrant foul - but no one was making the call.

I wished somehow and I still do that I could have traded places – somehow magically gone back to that Monday morning and traded places and gone for John so John could be here with you today. After all maybe this was a clerical error by Heaven, it was supposed to be Patrick Munley – the over the hill - out of shape guy out there running that beautiful morning – not John Patrick Munley, the world class athlete. If clerical errors happen in government, business and every other aspect of our lives - why not heaven? If only I could, I would correct the error but they tell me Heaven doesn't make errors and doesn't make exchanges.

As a parent one of the most difficult things for me to learn was the realization that we can't protect our children from all the difficult times, hardships, illnesses and diseases, misfortunes they may face. Try as we might, give advice and counsel as we might, do everything humanly possible we can imagine to try to protect them, to make sure they are ok – to try to insure their lives turn out well and they are happy - sometimes misfortune seems to strike for no apparent reason, and we feel helpless, feel like somehow and in some way we should have been able to prevent this terrible thing from happening – after all, isn't that our job, isn't that what parents are supposed to do, take care of their children and protect them even when they are 22 years old? I realize this is a question of balance, I know logically there is only so much parents can do – but the feeling and the desire to want to protect and take care of our children is so strong that it makes days like last Monday unbearable.

In my moments of most despair over the past few days I sometimes thought if this kind of thing is going to happen, if children are going to die without notice, without warning, if life isn't going to play by the rules, and if no one is there to call the flagrant foul, what's the sense, what's the meaning, I don't know if I can handle this.

But somehow in some of those very same moments I also realized that part of the answer is not simply in the moment of the loss itself but in taking the perspective of the past; and although the loss of John seems unbearable beyond words today, we, as a family, have also been blessed beyond words - blessed to have had the privilege of having John with us and a part of our family for the last 22 years, sharing all the wonderful times we have had as a family, sharing holidays, talks over the dinner table, going to swim meets, going canoeing, fishing, saving fish, catching frogs, going to the ocean to ride the waves, listening to John complain about poetry in English class and then later learning he had a poem published on how much he hated poetry, wondering as a family if John was serious or joking when planning on Frisbee Golf being his next sports career.

We simply would not trade those 22 years with John for anything – and nothing can ever take those 22 years and the memories and things we did together as a family away, and somehow, in spite of the unbearable pain of today, those memories and times together with John make it all so very worthwhile - we really are blessed as a family.

A big part of our family's life these past 20 years has been swimming. All five of the children swam. I always liked swimming because it is an inclusive sport. If a young person wants to try, is willing to put in the effort and go to practice and do their best they will make the high school team. Over the years of watching swimming I found that as good as any swimmer is, he or she will not be great without the right coaches. All of John's coaches, Jon Cook and Jeff Russell at the Portage Aquatic club, Vince Galent at South West Michigan Swimming; Dave Diget, Jim Schafer, Shelly Schafer, Ron Bramble, and Ty Parker at Portage Central; Richard Bader, Joel Eddy, John Narcy, Mary Ellen Wyden, Matt Gianiodis, Richard Mull, Jim Lutz and Christie Stefchunas at Michigan State, and Jon Urbanchek, Eric Namesnik and Stephanie Kerska at Club Wolverine, all were important figures in John's Life. We as a family owe each of these coaches and each of John's teammates a debt of gratitude that is not easily put into words. Hopefully the John Munley swimming memorial is just one small way to say thank you, to you and the sport he loved.

When John's swimming career ended a few weeks ago it was clear, that swimming was only the training ground for his future accomplishments in life. The place where he acquired self-confidence; learned to believe in himself, set goals and worked hard to achieve them. The place where he learned to cope with both success and failure; and most importantly the place where he learned to believe in his dreams. The fast swim times, the medals, the records, the Big Ten Championships, the Olympic Trials are all really nice but they are only one small part of what swimming was for John. Swimming was the place where he developed the character to work towards his dreams in life.

We as a family are very proud of John, proud of his accomplishments; proud of the way he dealt with his successes and failures, and proud of him as a person.

Coach Schafer put it so nicely when he said that John got the most out of his God-given ability more than any other swimmer he had known. John wanted to be the best he could be.

To our family, this was the part of what was so special about John and swimming – the striving to be the best he could be with his God given ability– his dedication to work and train hard, his courage to train and compete with some of the best in the world, his ability to imagine and envision new goals for himself, his setting high standards, his ability to cope with successes and disappointments, – his striving for goals others may not have thought of as possible, and his willingness to put in tremendous effort to try to achieve his goals and dreams. John was someone always going out after it - to the best of his ability. And perhaps that is one way he may best be remembered – as a young man who extended his abilities to their fullest potential in pursuit of his goals and his dreams.

I would like to conclude with a quotation by Theodore Roosevelt that I think applies to John, his life and his swimming career. This is something I read years ago that I lost track of but one that I recalled vividly in reflecting on John's life, and his swimming career. I never had a chance to share this with John but I would like to simply share it now with you and with John in John's memory.

"It is not the critic who counts; not the man who points out how the strong man stumbles, or where the doer of deeds could have done them better. The credit belongs to the man who is actually in the arena, whose face is marred by the dust and sweat and blood; who strives valiantly; who errs, and comes up short again and again, because there is no effort without error and shortcoming; but who does actually strive to do the deeds; who knows the great enthusiasms, the great devotion; who spends himself in a worthy cause; who at the best knows in the end the triumph of high achievement, and who at the worst if he fails, at least fails while daring greatly, so that his place shall never be with those cold and timid souls who know neither victory nor defeat." [1]

John, we love you.

Patrick Munley
May 5, 2001

---

[1] Theodore Roosevelt, Lecture on Citizenship in a Republic, the Sorbonne, Paris France, April 23, 1910.

Chapter 5

Life without John

It was hard to accept that John was gone. We never would have the opportunity to speak with him, to laugh with him, to tease him, to share life with him in all the ways we had. Never, never, for forever to see or be with John again – a cold simple fact so very obvious and yet so very hard to comprehend and to accept as final. There was no way to change what had happened, no way to go back, no way to make things right.

I never really came close to understanding how terrible losing a child was until we lost John. I guess like many people, I had an intellectual understanding of the nature of the loss. However, the actual experience of the loss was simply beyond words, far past anything I had ever imagined, well past everyday comprehension. Some years earlier, when all our children were still relatively young and at home, I had been diagnosed with cancer and underwent two major surgeries. At the time, the prognosis was somewhat uncertain with five years of medical follow-up and monthly x-rays required to be sure the surgery had been effective. When faced with the prospect of dying early the one thing that troubled me the most was the prospect of dying before the children had grown up. The prospect of not being around to take care of the children, to make sure they were provided for, to make sure they were alright, seemed overwhelming. The prospect of one of the children dying before me was something I never considered, since the prospect was so out of sync with the life-cycle.

Initially, I tried to comprehend and understand the pain of the loss and make some meaning out of it in a variety of ways. I wondered to myself whether or not part of the reason the loss was so painful was because John was 22 years old. We had 22 years with John, 22 years of memories and time together. Perhaps the amount of time together, the fact that he was just entering adulthood and finishing college, was the aspect that made the loss so much worse than perhaps it might otherwise be if a child was younger. Perhaps the loss of a younger child was easier to bear. I could not imagine anything feeling or being more terrible than what I was experiencing. However, I knew these thoughts and feelings were out of perspective, irrational and in no way true. The loss of a child at any age, is simply terrible beyond words - no matter the circumstances of the loss, it would be extremely painful and feel unbearable.

A few months after John had died a good friend of mine told me about a close young relative in his family who had been diagnosed with an illness that had the potential for being terminal. The family was having a difficult time accepting the situation. My perspective was that yes the situation was very, very difficult; but my feeling was that I would give anything, simply anything to just have John alive again for a few days, even knowing that he might be going to die in a short time. The opportunity to talk to him, to laugh, to joke, to hug him, even for a short time, was something so precious. I hoped my friend and his family realized how fortunate they were to still have their loved one alive, to be able to talk to her, laugh with her, with a chance and the hope, she would be fine.

What troubled me so much after John's death was my sense that somehow I was responsible. I should have been able to prevent what had happened to John. I am the father; I am responsible for his welfare and the welfare of all the children. Somehow I should have sensed and known there was something wrong. I knew he was big, the biggest of our children. His nickname was, "Big John", and many of the young children who knew and looked up to him called him "Big John." All the children had echocardiograms when they were young because one of John's siblings had a suspected mitral valve prolapse. All the children's echocardiograms and tests were normal. John's echocardiogram was normal. Why had I not thought to have John tested again when he was older? I thought I should have realized that John needed to be tested again when he got older. His involvement in sports, his performance at such a high level of competition contributed to his enlarged heart. Perhaps if I hadn't encouraged him to compete, maybe if I hadn't supported him to take the time in the summers to train for the Olympic trials, maybe his heart would not have become enlarged; maybe he would be alive today. Thoughts like these would go through my mind over and over, without any easy answers. I felt like I failed John, I let him down. A part of me knew these thoughts were in some respects irrational thoughts, yet another part of myself felt that somehow this should not have happened, John should not have died, I was the father. I was responsible.

The reminders of the loss of John were and are on a daily basis. Things like reading the newspapers and seeing stories of the deaths of other young people, watching television or movies with unanticipated scenes of death, dying or people being brought to emergency rooms all became reminders of John and what had happened. They were and are still difficult to encounter. Simple questions and social interactions from friends and acquaintances, such as "How are you?" "How is the family?" "How are the children?", often evoke deep and painful feelings. Such questions were often answered perfunctorily on a superficial level since it seemed like people could not bear to hear the truth. Or, if they could, it seemed impolite to really tell them what it feels like and what the experience really is like.

A few people would ask specifically about John and how the family was doing. These questions were often experienced as helpful in terms of reflecting genuine concern about the family and a respectful remembrance of John. But after six months specific questions about the family and John were very rare. I suspect most people simply felt uncomfortable mentioning John since they were not sure of the effect of the question. More general questions were difficult because the answer or the extent of the answer to be given was not clear. Also, if a superficial social answer was given, were we lying? Were we not being true to John? It seemed as if most people had moved on with their lives.

At some point following John's death I called the hospital for a copy of the final autopsy report and the secretary put me through to the Chief of the Office, the doctor who was responsible for signing the final Death Certificate. The process had taken somewhat longer due to the additional tests and procedures that were performed at Walter Reed Hospital. When I talked to the doctor he was very kind and very professional. After he clarified some information and was about to end the conversation he asked "How are you and your wife doing?" I replied that it was very difficult but I thought that we were doing alright. He responded that he knew how we felt. Sometimes when people tell others they know how they feel, there may be a ring of shallowness to the comment, but his comment was made with deep feeling and emotion. I did not say anything immediately in response because I was left wondering if he really could know how my wife and I felt. But then he went on to tell me that he and his wife had lost two children, both when they were adolescents. Clearly he knew what we were going through although I could only begin to imagine what he and his wife had been through in losing two children.

I took an airplane trip across country a few months after John had died. I was sitting in the aisle seat for the long flight. Next to me in the middle seat between the aisle and window sat a young woman with her infant on her lap. She was so happy with her young adorable baby. As the conversation touched upon children, and it was clear that I had some experience with children, she asked me how many children did I have? I answered five and told her about each one …. but left out the fact that John had recently died.

Perhaps I wanted to pretend for those few moments that he was still alive, maybe I couldn't bear to raise the possibility that children may die at a young age. Perhaps I didn't want to introduce any sadness into the moment. Over time I have realized that for me the correct answer to the question "How many children do you have?" is five; and I tell without hesitation about each child, including John and John's death. If I didn't speak about John, didn't tell the story, I felt very disrespectful to John.

One of my only initial respites from the pain of John being gone were dreams in which John would be very much alive. During the night before Fathers Day, 2001 I had the most vivid dream. We were living in our old house in West Orange, New Jersey. The house was an English Style Colonial with a red brick and white aluminum exterior and an Oak Wood Trim interior and brick fireplace in the living room. In the dream I was in the living room when I heard a knock on the front door. As I approached the door I looked out the window at the top of the door, but could see no one outside. I opened the door and there was John, at about age 4, standing in his old, hand-me-down, green overcoat, with wooden buttons connected by leather straps to the coat. He was smiling and looking adorable. I shouted "Mary Anne, Mary Anne, John is back!, John is here!" As I reached down and took John into my arms and hugged him as hard as I could, I said to him "John, John is that really you?" He shook his head to the left and the right as if to say no, and then spoke the words: "No, it is Big John." During the dream the happiness was real. John was alive again for a few moments. When I awoke I first felt this initial sense of happiness and relief feeling as if John were really alive. However, I quickly realized that it was only a dream and the happy feelings quickly subsided. Others in the family also had dreams about John being alive. Katie had told me about a dream she had that John had secretly gone on a trip to Las Vegas. He was really hiding there having the time of his life.

Hope cemetery, where John is buried, has become a place we visit often. I go there often, many times at night. Sometimes I will look up at the stars to see what our eternal resting place looks like from that spot. After the funeral and the service at the gravesite we left Winston there along with a Michigan State Flag. We later added an eternal solar candle, which burns continuously at night. To me it is an important symbol that the light of his life cannot be completely extinguished.

The swim team at Portage Central High School established a special award in John's memory for the high school swim team each year called the High Expectations Award. The award is given each year to a young man and young woman on the team in honor of John. The inscription on the award plaque reads:

"This award is given to a Portage Central swimmer/diver who strives to obtain the highest level of performance-- in and out of the pool-- through dedication, perseverance, sportsmanship, and leadership. John was a great swimmer, but he will always be remembered as a greater man."

Each year Elizabeth presents the award to the female swimmer who has been selected by the coaching staff to receive the award and Thomas presents the award to the male swimmer. The award has come to be a highly regarded honor by the swimmers with recipients proudly displaying their plaque at their graduation open houses. A parent of a recipient told the family how the award really turned her son around and changed his attitude toward swimming and success in school and college. There is a picture of John that hangs in the lobby of the Portage Central pool with the inscription: "NAFHE". Only the letters are inscribed on the picture so people will ask Coach Schafer what they stand for and he will tell them their meaning and about John Munley.

The family also placed a monument with a plaque about John at the site on Harrison Road in East Lansing where John collapsed. After John's death his brothers and sisters decided they wanted John to be remembered forever. They went to the University foundation office and established the John Munley Memorial Swimming Scholarship Endowment. The John Munley Swimming Scholarship is given each year at the MSU annual swim team dinner, the same dinner where John told me in his own way about his second tattoo of the Spartan S. The scholarship criteria, developed by his brothers and sisters, are that The John Munley Memorial Scholarship be awarded to:

> *The swimmer or diver who demonstrates an outstanding level of competitiveness, dedication to his sport, and loyalty to Michigan State University. The recipient continuously strives to make the most of his abilities, vigorously pursues his goals and dreams through training, and competes in a way that sets high standards for himself and his teammates. The awardee is a leader by example and demonstrates that hard work and dedication may lead to new levels of personal accomplishment; and represents the best of what athletics, sportsmanship, and Spartan Spirit are about at Michigan State University.*

In recent years a Masters outdoor long course swim meet has been held each June at Michigan State University in memory of John. The meet, organized by John's siblings, friends and swim team alumni, is attended by former team mates, friends, family and Masters swimmers from around Michigan and the Midwest. The meet affords an annual opportunity to gather in John's memory with proceeds going to help support the John Munley Memorial Scholarship.

Chapter 6

John's Writings

The poems and written journal entries by John presented in this chapter were part of a book of writings found by Elizabeth the evening before John's memorial service. These were written as part of a journal he kept for his Creative Writing class at Portage Central. Selections of the writings were read at his memorial service on May 4, 2001.

Rain

It was extreme. The rain was like a wall rushing towards me. It forced everyone to stop what they were doing and leave. Kids stopped playing, parents stopped talking to each other. They all went home except me. I laid down wearing nothing but my tomato red guard shorts and smoke tinted goggles. I waited. Then it came one drop at a time finally building up to the point where I had to blink my eyes from the force of the rain striking my goggles. I wasn't afraid of getting struck by lightning. I knew that the thing I enjoyed so much would not hurt me on a day like that day.

I stood up, ran, jumped. I felt like the wind was keeping me from falling down. I fell fast and yet hit the water softly barely making a splash. I felt like that I was suspended between two substances. The rain water on my body felt clean and pure. The pool water felt hard and gritty. I stayed in the pool for hours watching the rain trying to penetrate the surface. Finally the rain slowed down. Fewer and fewer drops hit the surface. I knew that I wouldn't feel the same about the rain. That day I learned that there are many types of rain with their own personalities. And since I left it hasn't rained.

death

john munley

The universe is said to be infinite, but currently scientists are baffled at the fact that there isn't enough matter to hold the universe together. Black holes could be an answer. A black hole is a dead star that is so dense its gravity is so strong it doesn't let light escape its pull. There's thought that there is a black hole outside the solar system. This is relevant to my thought on death because I believe that is where we go when we die.

My thought on the subject of what happens when you die is that when you die your soul is attracted to this black hole. Your soul consisting of our life energy or the force like in star wars. And our souls are conscious but not like we appear to be. The souls think of a reality and it exists for them. Much like a dream. Our whole existence is based on perception. What we perceive to be real is real. A good example of this is the economy. Look at a dollar bill, what's it worth? A dollar, a dollar is worth something because we believe it is worth something.

Lego Pieces

I remember; sand box, pool, tree, lake, minnows, gold fish, green basement, rickety stairs, flower wall paper, smurfs, He-man, GI Joe, train sets, sledding, snow, fights, ice skating, pond hockey, cheese lake, Nintendo, Atari, fishing, canoeing, red rider bebee guns, tree forts, blood, pain, hospital visits, bad teachers, good teachers, end of school, summer vacation, swimming, Jon Cook, brother beat downs, Christmas morning, Saturday morning cartoons, Night Court, Cheers, past my bed time, Legos, dirt trails, sand hill, death trails, bottle rockets, water balloon fights, playground football, chicken pox, green couch.

I hate it.

I hate it when you get hit in the head with a canned ham

I hate it when people stare and laugh at me saying
hey look at the
Idiot wearing clothes

I hate it when strangers go into your house and turn
all the furniture upside down

I hate it when I get Canadian coins from restaurants

I hate it when you're playing golf with old people
and they demand that I let them ride on the cart

I hate it when I go to school and get sexually
harassed by janitors

I hate welfare states

I hate it when you go to McDonald's and you ask to
see Ronald and they say he died from lung cancer.

Most of all I hate poetry.

alone but not lonely

--a collection of thoughts
by John Munley

the blue the purple the brown
it looks like i feel
the bottom looks so far away
i feel like a cloud flying
above a valley
wall

i feel like dropping something
i'm not alone how can i
i simply think about something
and there is no boredness
maybe for morons there's loneliness
wall

i feel no pressure
no nagging
no noise of people talking
just me and my thoughts
wall

it's hard to express thoughts
a lot harder than having them
people don't think like me
so how can i convey my thought to them
my thoughts are like a group of people talking
talking and sometimes being heard
wall

the problem with people
is the lack of thinking

No pain

John Munley

If I felt no pain
I wouldn't be human
always thinking
never to be

life hurts more
when I try to live
people are cruel
not thinking

self righteous people
listening to rap
thinking it's life's road map.
hurting those nearby

always looking straight
at life's road.
look to the side
and then they'll see

thoughts kept inside kill
trying seems worse
just wait and see
what it is to live

to live a life
of emptiness
never looking for
what they dream

Chapter 7

Remembering

A few days after John's death the Kalamazoo Gazette published an editorial on May 4, 2001, reprinted below:

"John Munley's Life Will Be Remembered
Portage, MSU swimmer left legacy of achievement"

Virtually all of us have an intellectual understanding of the fragility of life.

However, when tragedy strikes suddenly and takes away an apparently healthy and vigorous young man-whose achievements were but a sample of his potential- emotional comprehension is much more difficult.

On April 30, 22-year-old John Munley of Portage was jogging on the Michigan State University campus, where he had been a star swimmer. He collapsed and died. An autopsy showed that Munley had an enlarged heart.

Munley's death of course, shocked his loved ones, his friends and former teammates, both here and in the MSU community. Not only did he reach stardom as a Portage Central High School and four-year Spartan swimmer, but he also was an outstanding student aiming for a career in business.

Munley was the epitome of the kind of son any parent would be thrilled to have. Jim Lutz, Munley's college coach, said, "it was great to see him accomplish a lot of things, but there's so much more he'll never see".

That's certainly true. Yet during John Munley's relatively short time on earth, he lived his life to the fullest. In fact, in some respects he did as much or more in his 22 years than many people do in a normal lifespan.

Our sympathy goes out to his parents and other family members. What can't be taken away from them, however, are the memories of a wonderful son and brother."

The memories, the awards, the memorial scholarship, and the remembrances of John are all very important to the family. They do a great deal to help in remembering and honoring John, his life, respecting who he was as a person, what he stood for, what he accomplished. It is always important when people remember John. But paradoxically, in the very act of remembering and honoring him, we are faced with the painful reality that he is dead, and there is nothing we are able to do that can or will ever replace him. In remembering we are reminded he is no longer with us and will never be with us again, at least not in this life as we know it. No memory will ever be as vital, as vibrant, and as meaningful as actually having John with us. The loss is ever present, always with us in some form or another – at holidays, special occasions. Whenever the family is together, when the other children in the family get married, have children of their own, or are together on other special occasions, there is always the reality that John is not present. I think everyone is somewhat aware and has the thought that 'John would have loved to be here for this', or, 'I wonder what John would say if he were here'.

I think this is the paradox that sometimes holds people back at times from asking families or parents about the lost child or about how the family is doing following the death. A person may care a great deal, have the instinct to ask or inquire about the family and the child who is lost, but hold back in asking because they do not wish to remind the family of the loss, and in so doing perhaps cause some pain or discomfort. Yet in my experience it always means a great deal when people ask about the family, acknowledge the anniversary of John's death or remember him in some way. These inquiries are always appreciated. While the act of remembering may at times cause some pain and discomfort, there is also much joy and happiness in remembering him. Inquiries by others are always appreciated because they reaffirm John's life, reaffirm that others remember him and think about him, and that others still feel a bond to him.

Some years ago I had the opportunity to hear Gerda Weissman Klein, a Holocaust survivor and author, speak. She was a concentration camp survivor and lost her parents and her brother during the Holocaust. She spoke of her experiences as a child, her experiences during the war and the loss of her family in the camps. At the conclusion of her talk, she asked those present to do something that I will not forget; something I think about at times when reflecting upon John. She asked everyone when they went home that evening to approach their homes very slowly …. to stop for a few minutes and to look at their homes, and think about the people who were inside ….. to look at the lights and reflect on the warmth within …. and to take some time to truly appreciate the warmth in the home and everyone and all that we have there.

Even amidst the pain of the loss of John, there is something very special about remembering him, something wonderful about honoring him in the little ways that we do. There is something breathtaking about being so aware that the love we have for him is still so present after all these years. Even though he is not physically present with us

79

today, his warmth is still present. In the very act of remembering him, there is a special connection and bond that takes place, a special connection that seems to give meaning to his life, to our lives as a family, a special bond that transcends the limitations of the physical existence of life as we typically know and experience it on a day-to-day basis. A bond that somehow says to everyone and everything, that even in the face of death, life is worthwhile beyond measure. Even in the face of death, relationships matter and are important and somehow these connections continue and remain meaningful across the space and time of the Universe. Even with death … nothing may take away the bonds between people who love and care for each other.